FACT CAT

SEASONS

Izzi Howell

WAYLAND
www.waylandbooks.co.uk

FACT CAT

Get your paws on this fantastic new mega-series from Wayland!

Join our Fact Cat on a journey of fun learning about every subject under the sun!

First published in Great Britain in 2016 by Wayland
Copyright © Wayland 2016

ISBN: 978 0 7502 9696 0
10 9 8 7 6 5 4 3 2 1

Wayland
An imprint of Hachette Children's Group
Part of Hodder & Stoughton
Carmelite House
50 Victoria Embankment
London EC4Y 0DZ

An Hachette UK Company
www.hachette.co.uk
www.hachettechildrens.co.uk

A catalogue for this title is available from
the British Library
Printed and bound in China

Produced for Wayland by
White-Thomson Publishing Ltd
www.wtpub.co.uk

Editor: Izzi Howell
Design: Clare Nicholas
Fact Cat illustrations: Shutterstock/Julien Troneur
Other illustrations: Stefan Chabluk
Consultant: Karina Philip

The author, Izzi Howell, is a writer and editor specialising in children's educational publishing.

The consultant, Karina Philip, is a teacher and a primary literacy consultant with an MA in creative writing.

FACT CAT FACT

There is a question for you to answer on each spread in this book. You can check your answers on page 24.

CONTENTS

WHAT ARE SEASONS?

There are four seasons in a year: spring, summer, autumn and winter. In each season, we can see changes in nature and the weather.

Plants change with the seasons.

cherry tree branch in spring

beech branch in summer

maple leaves in autumn

oak branches in winter

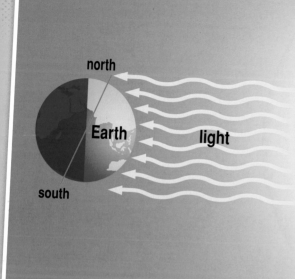

north

Earth

light

south

Sun

In space, the Earth **orbits** the Sun. Seasons happen because the Earth is **tilted** to one side as it goes around the Sun.

When one part of the Earth is tilted towards the Sun, it is summer there. It is winter in the part of the Earth that is tilted away from the Sun.

FACT CAT FACT

It takes one year for the Earth to orbit the Sun. How many days are there in a year?

AROUND THE WORLD

An imaginary line, called the **equator**, splits the Earth into two parts – the northern and southern **hemispheres**. The hemispheres have opposite seasons. When it is summer in the north, it is winter in the south.

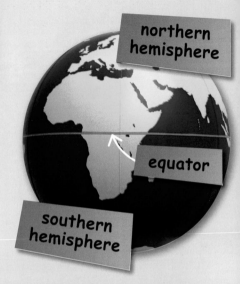

northern hemisphere

equator

southern hemisphere

In Australia, the best time to visit the beach is during the summer months of December, January and February. Which hemisphere is Australia in?

In **tropical** areas close to the equator, there are only two seasons – the wet season and the dry season. In most tropical places, the **climate** is warm all year round.

These Indian tea pickers are using umbrellas to keep dry in the wet season. Tea grows well in warm, rainy weather.

FACT CAT FACT

Many rainforests are found close to the equator because they grow well in hot, wet climates.

SPRING

In spring, the weather is often rainy and windy. After a cold winter, the **temperature** starts to get warmer. New plants grow and flowers start to **bloom**.

Daffodil bulbs are planted in the winter.

Daffodils are one of the first flowers to bloom in spring.

Many animals give birth to their **young** in spring. **Female** birds lay eggs in nests. Later, young birds (chicks) hatch from the eggs.

Female sheep often give birth to more than one lamb. What is another word for a female sheep?

FACT CAT FACT

Lambs take their first steps only an hour after being born!

SUMMER

The weather in summer is usually warm and sunny. It doesn't rain very often.

Children often play outside during the summer.

10

Many flowers bloom in summer. Insects, such as bees and butterflies, collect **nectar** from flowers. Towards the end of summer, fruit starts to grow on plants and trees.

This honeybee is sucking nectar from a flower with its tongue. Which sweet food do honeybees make from nectar?

FACT CAT FACT

Honeybees beat their wings 200 times every second when they are flying!

AUTUMN

In autumn, the weather starts to get colder. Farmers **harvest** plants, such as corn and wheat, that have been growing all summer.

This machine, called a combine harvester, is picking wheat. Find out the name of two foods that are made from wheat.

Many animals, such as woodmice and squirrels, collect fruit and nuts in autumn. They hide the food in their nests or **bury** it under the ground. They eat this food later, in winter.

Red squirrels often hide nuts in holes in tree trunks.

FACT CAT FACT

In autumn, some red squirrels hang mushrooms in trees to dry out. They eat the dry mushrooms in winter.

WINTER

Winter is the coldest season. Lakes and rivers sometimes **freeze**. Snow and **hail** fall from clouds in the sky.

Icicles are made when dripping water freezes into ice. At which temperature does water freeze?

FACT CAT FACT

No two snowflakes look the same! Each one is different.

Some plants die in winter. Others rest underground until spring. A few animals, such as bats and hedgehogs, **hibernate** during the winter. They wake up in spring when the weather gets warmer.

Dormice hibernate for up to six months.

Deer do not hibernate in winter.

TYPES OF TREES

There are two types of trees
- **deciduous** and **evergreen**.
Deciduous trees look
different in every season.

In autumn, the leaves on
deciduous trees change
colour and start to fall
to the ground.

In winter, deciduous trees look
dead because they have lost all of
their leaves. However, they are
still alive and new leaves will grow
on their branches in spring.

The leaves on evergreen trees are green all year round, even in winter. Can you tell which trees are evergreen and which trees are deciduous in this picture?

Evergreen trees look the same in every season. They slowly lose their leaves and grow new ones throughout the year.

FACT CAT FACT

Many evergreen trees, such as fir and pine trees, have spiky leaves called needles rather than broad leaves.

DAY AND NIGHT

The length of day and night changes with the seasons. In winter, there are more hours of darkness than of daylight.

In this Norwegian town, the sun sets early in winter. It is dark for most of the afternoon.

As winter turns into spring, the sun starts to rise earlier and set later. By summer, the day is longer than the night.

As summer turns into autumn, the sun begins to rise later and set earlier.

FACT CAT FACT

North Pole

South Pole

At the Earth's **poles**, it doesn't get dark during the summer. The sun doesn't set for several months. How many hours of darkness are there at the poles in winter?

MIGRATION

Every autumn, monarch butterflies migrate from North America to Mexico so that they are in a warm place during the winter. They fly back home in spring.

Some animals move to another part of the world at the same time every year. This is called **migration**. Animals migrate to find food, to have young or to find warmer weather.

North America

Mexico

Some animals, such as grey whales and salmon, migrate across oceans and along rivers. Other animals, such as zebras and reindeer, migrate across the land.

Up to **1.5 million** wildebeest migrate around the **savannahs** of Africa in May and June, looking for grass to eat. Which other animals migrate with the wildebeests?

FACT CAT **FACT**

Arctic terns have the longest migration of any bird. Every year, they travel nearly 80,000 kilometres, flying from the North Pole to the South Pole and back again!

QUIZ Try to answer the questions below. Look back through the book to help you. Check your answers on page 24.

1 Seasons happen because the Earth is tilted as it orbits the Sun. True or not true?

a) true

b) not true

2 What is the name of a young sheep?

a) puppy

b) chick

c) lamb

3 Which season has the warmest weather?

a) summer

b) winter

c) autumn

4 Deciduous trees die in winter. True or not true?

a) true

b) not true

5 In winter, the sun rises late and sets early. True or not true?

a) true

b) not true

6 Which of these animals does not migrate?

a) monarch butterfly

b) dormouse

c) grey whale

GLOSSARY

bloom when a plant blooms, its flowers open

bury to put something in a hole in the ground and cover it

climate the most common weather in an area

deciduous a type of tree with leaves that change colour and fall off in winter

equator an imaginary line around the middle of the Earth

evergreen a type of tree that doesn't lose its leaves in winter

female describes an animal that can give birth to young or lay eggs from which young will hatch

freeze when a liquid turns hard and solid because of the cold

hail small pieces of frozen rain that fall from the sky

harvest to cut and collect crops when they are ripe

hemisphere one half of the Earth. The northern hemisphere lies above the equator, and the southern hemisphere lies below the equator.

hibernate to sleep all winter and wake up in spring

icicle a long thin piece of ice that hangs from something

migration when an animal travels from one place to another at the same time each year

million one thousand thousand (1,000,000)

nectar a sweet liquid made by plants

orbit to travel around something in a circular movement

poles the northernmost and southernmost points on Earth

savannah a flat area of land covered in grass and some trees

temperature how hot or cold something is

tilted describes something that is not straight and leans to one side

tropical describes a place that is hot and wet

young an animal's babies

INDEX

ANSWERS

Pages 4–20

Page 5: 365 days or 366 days in a leap year

Page 6: Southern hemisphere

Page 9: Ewe

Page 11: Honey

Page 12: Some foods include bread, pasta and cakes.

Page 14: 0° Celsius

Page 17: The trees at the front of the picture are evergreen and the trees at the back are deciduous.

Page 19: 24 hours

Page 21: Zebras and gazelles

Quiz answers

1   true

2   c - lamb

3   a - summer

4   not true – they lose their leaves, but they do not die.

5   true

6   b - dormouse

OTHER TITLES IN THE FACT CAT SERIES...

WAYLAND
www.waylandbooks.co.uk